CHOCOLATE
TEMPTATIONS

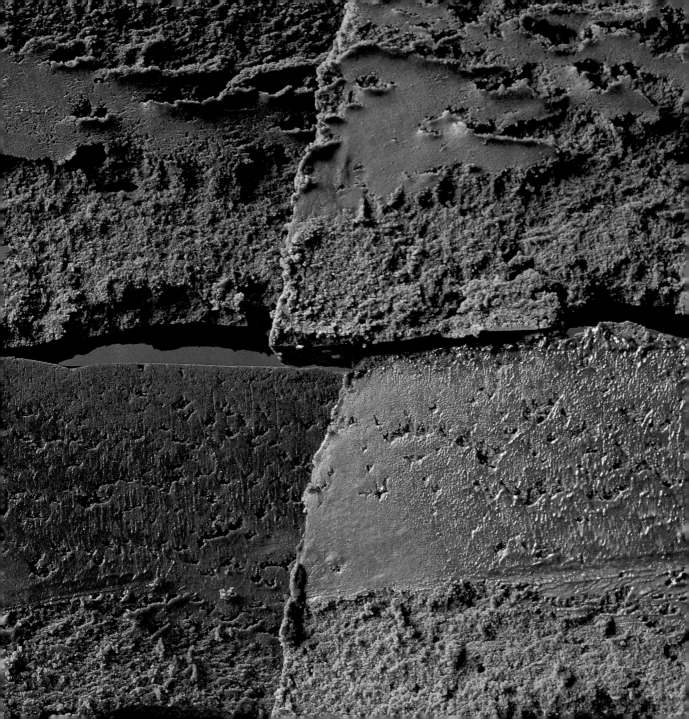

CHOCOLATE
TEMPTATIONS

LINDA COLLISTER
Photography by
Patrica de Villiers

RYLAND
PETERS
& SMALL

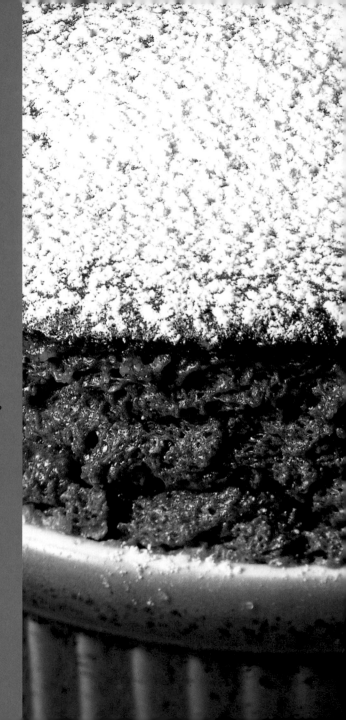

Art Director **Jacqui Small**

Art Editor **Penny Stock**

Editor **Elsa Petersen-Schepelern**

Photography **Patrice de Villiers**

Food Stylist **Linda Collister**

Stylist **Penny Markham**

Production **Kate Mackillop**

For Emily

Notes: Ovens should be preheated to the specified temperature—if using a fan-assisted oven, adjust time and temperature according to the manufacturer's instructions.

First published in the USA as *Basic Baking Chocolate* in 1997
This edition published in 2000 by
Ryland Peters & Small, Inc.,
150 West 56th Street, Suite 6303, New York, N.Y. 10019

10 9 8 7 6 5 4 3 2 1

Text © Linda Collister 1997
Design and photographs © Ryland Peters & Small 1997

Printed and bound in China by Toppan Printing Co.

ISBN 1-84172-090-9

A CIP catalog record for this book is available from the Library of Congress

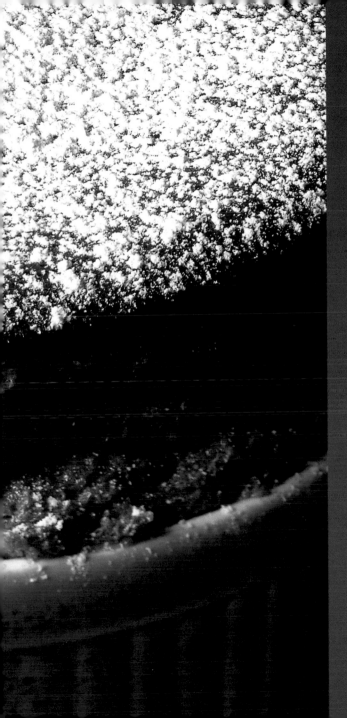

CONTENTS

baking with
chocolate

Eating chocolate is **pure joy**, cooking with it a delight, even smelling it is bewitching, but buying it shakes my faith in human nature.

The best chocolate is wonderful, but most is not worth buying and most people buy terrible stuff. Good quality bittersweet chocolate will taste **smooth** not greasy, **bitter** not raw, **intense** not oversweet, with a **long finish,** not an excessively sweet aftertaste.

But how do you know good quality? Price is not a reliable guide—in fact supermarkets' **own brands** are usually excellent and are a good bargain when buying in bulk for cooking.

The quality and taste of chocolate is determined by the quantity and quality of the **cocoa solids**—the dry solids plus the added cocoa butter—used in its production. The quantity of solids, at least, is indicated on the package.

American bittersweet chocolate or European **dark cooking chocolate** such as Lindt is best for baking. Bittersweet has around 35 percent cocoa solids, whereas Lindt—which is widely available in good supermarkets and specialty shops—has up to 55 percent. Couverture chocolate produces a very glossy surface, and is used by professional bakers.

The raw material for chocolate is the cocoa bean, found in the large yellow-green fruits of the *Theobroma cacao* tree which grows only within 20 degrees north or south of the equator. Each tree yields enough beans to make around 5 lb. of chocolate each year.

The best chocolate is made from a **blend of beans**—each type has its own individual character and color, ranging from pale coffee through to dark mahogany brown.

Store chocolate well away from other foods in an airtight container in a **cool, dry place,** because it can easily be tainted by other flavors. Avoid storing chocolate below 55°F, or in the fridge, as beads of moisture will form when you bring it to room temperature.

Don't store in a hot kitchen (85°F or above) or it will develop a white bloom as the cocoa butter comes to the surface. The bloom does not affect its taste however—it can still used for cooking. Chocolate begins melting at 85°F (that's why it melts in the mouth) and burns at 228°F. Melt it **slowly and gradually** as it easily becomes overheated and scorched, and turns into an unusable solid mass. Chop it into evenly sized pieces so it melts at the same rate. Place in a shallow, heatproof bowl set over a pan of steaming hot, not boiling, water. The water must not touch the base of the bowl, and no drop of water or steam should touch the chocolate or it will seize up. Stir **frequently**, and remove from the heat as soon as it melts.

INCREDIBLE **CAKES**

almond
chocolate kugelhopf

2⅔ cups white bread flour

½ teaspoon sea salt

¾ cake compressed yeast

5 tablespoons sugar

¾ cup plus 1 tablespoon
skim milk, tepid

3 eggs, beaten

2½ oz. bittersweet chocolate

7 tablespoons sweet butter

½ cup slivered or flaked almonds

Nut Coating:

1¾ tablespoons sweet butter

½ cup slivered or flaked almonds

confectioners' sugar, for dusting

one 9-inch kugelhopf mold

Makes 1 large cake

To use easy-blend dried yeast, mix 1 package with 1 cup of the flour. Mix in the sugar and milk and let rise for 30 minutes. Make a well in the remaining flour, add the salt, add the yeast liquid and eggs and proceed with the recipe.

To make the nut coating, soften the butter and spread thickly inside the kugelhopf mold, then press the almonds all around. Chill while preparing the dough.

To make the dough, mix the flour and salt in a large mixing bowl, then make a well in the center.

Crumble the yeast into a small bowl, then cream to a smooth liquid with the sugar and milk. Pour into the well, and work in enough flour to make a thick batter.

Cover with a damp cloth, and leave at normal room temperature for 30 minutes. The batter should look bubbly.

Add the eggs to the yeast liquid, stir until combined, then gradually beat in the flour to make a soft and very sticky dough. Beat the dough in the bowl with your hand or with the dough hook in an electric mixer for about 5 minutes or until it becomes firmer, smooth, very elastic, and shiny.

Chop the chocolate and soften the butter. Add to the bowl, together with the almonds, and work in until thoroughly incorporated. When evenly mixed, carefully spoon the soft dough into the prepared mold (it should be half full).

Cover the mold with a damp cloth and let rise at cool to normal room temperature until the dough has almost doubled in size and has risen to about 1 inch below the rim of the mold—about 1 hour.

Bake in a preheated oven at 400°F for 45 minutes or until the cake is golden brown and a skewer inserted midway between the outer edge and inner tube comes out clean. Let cool for

1 minute, then carefully unmold onto a wire rack and let cool completely. Serve dusted with confectioners' sugar.

Store in an airtight container and eat within 3 days or freeze for up to 1 month. It can be lightly toasted under a broiler.

Variations:

Marbled Kugelhopf

Replace ⅓ cup of the white bread flour with ½ cup sifted unsweetened cocoa and 2 tablespoons sugar. Replace the 2½ oz. bittersweet chocolate with a similar quantity of white chocolate, coarsely chopped. Proceed as in the main recipe.

Golden Raisin Kugelhopf

Replace ⅓ cup of the white bread flour with ½ cup sifted unsweetened cocoa and 2 tablespoons sugar. Replace the 2½ oz. bittersweet chocolate with a similar quantity of golden raisins or raisins. Proceed as in the main recipe.

Note: *Both cocoa variations of this recipe are delicious toasted and spread with peanut butter.*

This **pretty,** *yeast coffee-time cake is made in a traditional earthenware mold, a tube pan, or non-stick ring mold. Serve it either* **plain** *or toasted.*

A great combination of ginger in syrup and bittersweet chocolate.

chocolate gingerbread

5½ oz. bittersweet chocolate

1⅓ sticks (¾ cup plus
1 tablespoon) sweet butter,
at room temperature

¾ cup sugar

3 large eggs, separated

½ cup plus 1 tablespoon
ground almonds

¾ cup plus 1½ tablespoons
self-rising flour

1 tablespoon unsweetened cocoa

3 pieces preserved ginger,
chopped, and 2 tablespoons
syrup from jar

Chocolate Topping:

1½ oz. bittersweet chocolate

1 tablespoon sweet butter

1 piece of preserved ginger,
sliced, and 1 tablespoon syrup
from the jar, to finish

one loaf pan, 8½ x 4½ x 3 inches,
greased and lined with
baking parchment

Chop the chocolate and melt very gently melt in a heatproof bowl set over a pan of steaming water. Stir until smooth, remove from the heat, and let cool. Using an electric mixer or wooden spoon, beat the butter until creamy, then gradually beat in the sugar. Beat until light and fluffy, then beat in the egg yolks one at a time, beating well after each addition. Beat in the cooled chocolate, then sift the almonds, flour, and cocoa into the bowl. Add the chopped ginger and syrup, and fold in using a large metal spoon.

Whisk the egg whites until stiff peaks form, then fold into the mixture in 3 batches.

Spoon the mixture into the prepared pan and smooth the surface. Bake in a preheated oven at 375°F for about 40 minutes or until a skewer inserted into the center of the cake comes out clean. Leave for 5 minutes, then turn out onto a wire rack and let cool completely.

To make the topping, chop the chocolate and melt it with the butter and ginger syrup in a heatproof bowl set over a pan of steaming water. Stir until smooth, then spoon over the top of the cake. When almost set, decorate with finely sliced, diced, or grated preserved ginger.

Store in an airtight container and eat within 1 week—it improves in taste after several days. If undecorated, it can be frozen for up to 1 month.

marbled fudge cake

½ stick (¼ cup) sweet butter

3 oz. graham crackers, crushed

Chocolate Mixture:

3 tablespoons sweet butter

4 oz. bittersweet chocolate

2 large eggs

¾ cup sugar

½ cup all-purpose flour

a pinch of salt

½ teaspoon baking powder

2–3 drops real vanilla extract

2 oz. walnut pieces or pecans

Vanilla Mixture:

1¾ tablespoons sweet butter

½ teaspoon real vanilla extract

⅓ cup cream cheese

4½ tablespoons sugar

1 large egg, beaten

1 tablespoon all-purpose flour

one 8¼-inch springform
pan, greased

Makes 1 cake (16 slices)

To make the base, melt the butter and mix with the cracker crumbs, then press into the base of thé pan to make a thin, even layer. Chill while preparing the filling.

To make the chocolate mixture, dice the butter and bring to room temperature. Chop the chocolate and melt gently in a heatproof bowl set over a pan of barely simmering water. Stir until smooth, remove from the heat, and stir in the butter.

In another bowl beat the eggs and sugar with a wooden spoon until frothy. Sift the flour, salt, and baking powder into the bowl and stir well. Add the melted chocolate mixture and the vanilla. Chop the nuts, add to the bowl, and mix well. Spread over the base.

To make the vanilla mixture, bring the butter to room temperature, then beat until creamy using a wooden spoon or electric mixer. Beat in the vanilla and cream cheese until the mixture is light and fluffy. Gradually beat in the sugar, then the egg. Add the flour and stir well. Spoon on top of the chocolate and swirl the tip of a knife through the mixtures giving a marbled effect.

Bake in a preheated oven at 350°F for about 25 minutes until just firm. Let cool in the pan before unmolding. Serve at room temperature. Store in an airtight container and eat within 5 days, or freeze for up to 1 month.

*This cake **improves** in flavor for several days after baking.*

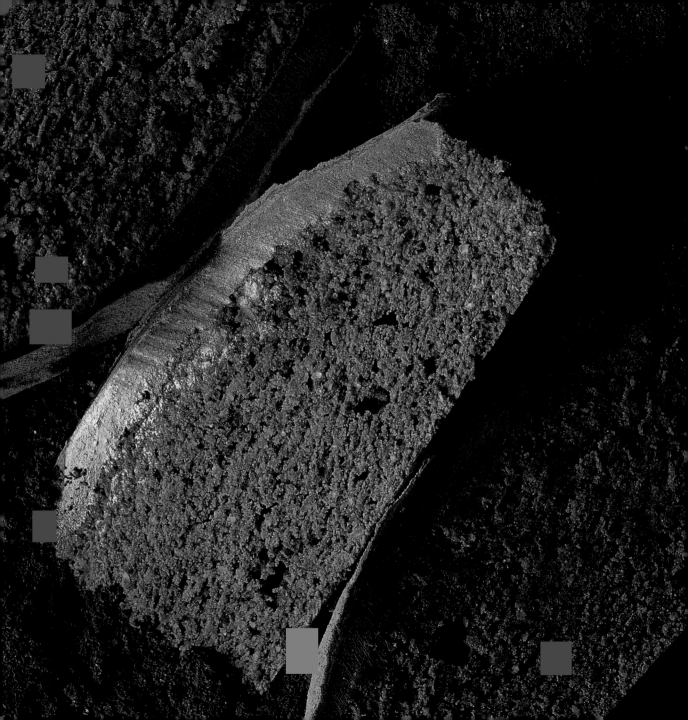

espresso cake

Sift the flour with the cocoa, salt, coffee, and ground almonds. In a mixing bowl, beat the butter until creamy using a wooden spoon or electric mixer. Gradually beat in the sugar. When light and fluffy, beat in the eggs, 1 tablespoon at a time. Carefully fold in the dry ingredients, hot water, and alcohol. Spoon into the prepared springform pan and smooth the surface. Bake in a preheated oven at 350°F for about 40 minutes, or until a skewer inserted into the center of the cake comes out clean. Carefully loosen the cake then unclip the pan. Let cool on a wire rack. To make the frosting, heat the cream until scalding hot, then remove from the heat and add the chocolate and coffee or alcohol. Leave until completely melted then stir gently. When cool and thick enough to spread, use to cover the top and sides of the cake. Leave until set, then store in an airtight container overnight before cutting. Eat within 1 week, or freeze for up to 1 month.

Finely _ground_ espresso coffee rather than liquid coffee may seem a rather odd ingredient for this _moist_ cake—but it tastes extraordinarily good!

1½ cups self-rising flour

1 cup minus 1 tablespoon unsweetened cocoa

a pinch of salt

1 tablespoon very finely ground espresso coffee

1⅓ cups ground almonds

2 sticks (1 cup) sweet butter

1 cup plus 2½ tablespoons superfine or granulated sugar

4 large eggs, beaten

3 tablespoons very hot water

1 tablespoon coffee liqueur or brandy (optional)

Chocolate Frosting:

⅔ cup heavy cream

5½ oz. bittersweet chocolate, chopped

1 tablespoon very strong black coffee, coffee liqueur, or brandy

one 9½-inch springform pan, greased and lined with baking parchment

Makes 1 cake

Make this soft, moist, flourless cake with macadamias, pecans, walnuts, almonds, or hazelnuts.

fudgy nut cake

12 oz. bittersweet chocolate

1½ sticks (¾ cup)
sweet butter, diced

½ cup unsweetened cocoa, sifted

3½ oz. mixture of nuts

5 large eggs

1 teaspoon real vanilla extract

1¼ cups sugar

confectioners' sugar and
unsweetened cocoa, for dusting

one 8½-inch springform pan,
greased and lined with
baking parchment

Makes 1 cake

Chop the chocolate and put into a heatproof bowl together with the diced butter. Set over a pan of steaming water and stir frequently until melted and smooth. Remove from the heat, stir in the cocoa, then let cool.

Meanwhile, coarsely chop the nuts. Put the eggs, vanilla, and sugar into a large heatproof bowl and beat briefly until frothy. Set the bowl over a pan of steaming water—the water should not touch the base of the bowl. Using an electric egg beater, beat the mixture until it is very pale and thick—when the beater is lifted it should leave a visible ribbon-like trail.

Remove the bowl from the heat, and beat for a couple of minutes so the mixture cools. Using a large metal spoon, carefully fold in the chocolate mixture, followed by the nuts. When thoroughly combined, spoon into the prepared springform pan and smooth the surface.

Bake in a preheated oven at 350°F for about 35 minutes or until firm to the touch but moist inside (do not overcook or the cake will be dry and hard to slice).

Let cool in the pan, then turn out and serve, dusted with cocoa and confectioners' sugar.

Store in an airtight container and eat within 1 week. It does not freeze well.

Rum-soaked golden raisins, butter, sugar, flour, and cocoa—a terrific combination. *Don't* worry if the fruit sinks during baking.

chocolate pound cake

3 oz. golden raisins

3 tablespoons rum

4 large eggs, at room temperature

about 2 sticks (1 cup) plus 2 tablespoons sweet butter, at room temperature

about 1¼ cups superfine or granulated sugar

½ cup unsweetened cocoa

about 1⅓ cups self-rising flour

a pinch of salt

one 2 lb. loaf pan, lined with a double thickness of greased wax paper

Makes 1 large cake

Soak the golden raisins in the rum, cover, and leave overnight. The next day, weigh the 4 eggs together and use exactly the same weight of butter and sugar.

Add to the cocoa enough of the flour to make the same weight. Sift the cocoa, flour, and salt twice.

Put the measured soft butter in the bowl of an electric mixer and beat until creamy. Gradually beat in the measured sugar. After the last addition beat the mixture until it becomes very white and light in texture.

Beat the eggs in a separate bowl, then beat into the butter mixture, 1 tablespoon at a time, beating well after each addition. Using a large metal spoon, fold in the sifted flour mixture very gently. When thoroughly combined, fold in the golden raisins and any rum left in the bowl.

Spoon into the prepared pan and smooth the surface. Bake in a preheated oven at 400°F for 40 to 50 minutes or until a cocktail stick or skewer comes out clean.

Cool the cake in the pan for a couple of minutes, then lift it out and peel off the paper. Let cool completely on a wire rack. Store in an airtight container and eat within 1 week, or freeze for up to 1 month.

devil's food cake

Chop the chocolate and gently melt with the butter, sugar, and syrup in a heavy pan over low heat, stirring frequently. Remove from the heat and let cool.

Sift the flour, cocoa, and baking soda into a mixing bowl and make a well in the center. Pour in the melted mixture, stir gently, then add the eggs, vanilla, and milk. Beat very gently with a wooden spoon until well mixed.

Spoon the mixture into the prepared pans and spread evenly. Bake in a preheated oven at 325°F for about 15 to 20 minutes until just firm to the touch. Let cool, then turn out of the pans.

To make the frosting, chop the chocolate. Heat the milk and sugar, stirring until dissolved, then boil rapidly for 1 minute until syrupy. Remove from the heat and stir in the chocolate. When melted and smooth, stir in the butter and vanilla. Let cool, stirring occasionally, then beat well until very thick.

Spread one-third of this mixture onto one of the cakes and set the second on top. Spread the rest of the mixture evenly over the top and sides. Leave in a cool spot (not the fridge) until set. Store in an airtight container and eat within 5 days. The undecorated cakes can be frozen for up to 1 month.

An unusual, *quick*, and *easy* method that produces a very dark cake—yet *light* and full of flavor.

3 oz. bittersweet chocolate

1 stick (½ cup) sweet butter

7 tablespoons dark brown sugar

1 tablespoon golden syrup* or dark corn syrup

1 cup plus 2 tablespoons all-purpose flour

¼ cup unsweetened cocoa

½ teaspoon baking soda

2 large eggs, beaten

½ teaspoon real vanilla extract

½ cup minus 1 tablespoon milk

Chocolate Frosting:

2½ oz. bittersweet chocolate

⅔ cup whole milk

½ cup sugar

½ stick (¼ cup) sweet butter, at room temperature

½ teaspoon real vanilla extract

two 7-inch sandwich pans, greased and lined with baking parchment

Makes 1 cake

Available in larger supermarkets.

CREATIVE COOKIES

chocolate crackles

4 oz. bittersweet chocolate,
coarsely chopped

1 stick (½ cup) sweet butter,
diced, at room temperature

1 large egg

2–3 drops real vanilla extract

¾ cup plus 2 tablespoons
light brown sugar

1 cup plus 2 tablespoons
self-rising flour

½ teaspoon baking soda

about 2 tablespoons
confectioners' sugar, for coating

several baking trays, greased

Makes about 28

Melt the chopped chocolate gently in a heatproof bowl set over a pan of barely simmering water, stirring frequently. Remove the bowl from the heat and gradually stir in the butter. In another bowl, beat the egg and vanilla until frothy using a wire whisk or electric mixer. Gradually beat in the sugar, followed by the chocolate mixture.

Sift the flour and baking soda into the bowl, then stir in to make a firm dough. In hot weather or if the dough seems sticky, wrap it and chill for 15 minutes.

Using your hands, roll the dough into walnut-sized balls. Roll each ball in confectioners' sugar, then arrange, spaced well apart, on the prepared baking trays.

Bake in a preheated oven at 400°F for about 10 to 12 minutes until just firm.

Cool for 1 minute until firm enough to transfer to a wire rack to cool completely.

Store in an airtight container and eat within 1 week, or freeze for up to 1 month.

These biscuits **crack** *and spread in the oven—finish with a dusting of confectioners' sugar to make them look even more* **dramatic.**

Cut these shortbread cookies into any **pretty** shape, then bake, cool, and **dip** in chocolate.

cinnamon
chocolate stars

Using a wooden spoon or electric mixer beat the butter until creamy. Gradually beat in the sugar. When the mixture is pale and fluffy, sift the flour, salt, cinnamon, and rice flour into the bowl and mix. When the mixture comes together, turn it onto a lightly floured surface and knead lightly and briefly to make a smooth, but not sticky dough. In hot weather, or if the dough feels sticky, wrap it and chill until firm.
Roll out the dough to about ¼ inch thick and cut out shapes with the cutter. Gently knead together the trimmings, then re-roll and cut more stars.
Arrange the stars slightly apart on the prepared baking trays. Prick with a fork and chill for about 15 minutes.
Bake the cookies in a preheated oven at 350°F for about 12 to 15 minutes or until firm and barely colored.
Let cool on the baking trays for a couple of minutes until firm enough to transfer to a wire cooling rack.
When completely cold, gently melt the chocolate in a small heatproof bowl set over a pan of steaming water. Stir until smooth, then remove the bowl from the heat. Dip the points of the stars in to the melted chocolate, then leave to set on waxed paper, non-stick parchment, or a wire rack.
When firm, store in an airtight container and eat within 3 days. Undecorated cookies can be frozen for up to 1 month.

1½ sticks (¾ cup) plus
1 tablespoon sweet butter,
at room temperature

7 tablespoons sugar

1½ cups all-purpose flour

a good pinch of salt

1 teaspoon ground cinnamon

5 tablespoons rice flour
or cornstarch

2 oz. bittersweet chocolate,
to finish

one star-shaped cookie cutter

several baking trays, greased

Makes 30

black and white
cookies

1 stick (½ cup) sweet butter, at room temperature

7 tablespoons light brown sugar

1 large egg, beaten

6½ tablespoons self-rising flour

½ teaspoon baking powder

a pinch of salt

½ teaspoon real vanilla extract

1½ cups rolled oats

6½ oz. bittersweet chocolate, chopped into chunks

several baking trays, greased

Makes about 24

Beat the butter until creamy using a wooden spoon or electric mixer. Add the sugar and beat until light and creamy. Gradually beat in the egg, and beat well after the last addition. Sift the flour with the baking powder and salt into the mixing bowl, add the vanilla extract and oats, and stir in. When thoroughly combined, stir in the chocolate chunks. Put heaped teaspoons of the mixture, spaced well apart, onto the prepared trays, then bake in a preheated oven at 350°F for 12 to 15 minutes until golden and just firm.

Let cool on the trays for a couple of minutes until firm enough to transfer to a wire rack.

Let cool completely, then store in an airtight container. Eat within 1 week or freeze for up to 1 month.

*Make chocolate chips by chopping good **bittersweet** chocolate into large chunks—the flavor is far **superior** to the commercial chocolate chips.*

Chocolate chip cookies with a difference—the dough is flavored with **melted** *bittersweet chocolate plus chocolate* **chunks.**

giant double chocolate nut cookies

5 oz. bittersweet chocolate, chopped

7 tablespoons sweet butter, at room temperature

6½ tablespoons superfine or granulated sugar

6½ tablespoons dark brown sugar

1 large egg, beaten

½ teaspoon real vanilla extract

1 cup all-purpose flour

a pinch of salt

½ teaspoon baking powder

2 oz. pecans or walnuts, chopped

3½ oz. unsweetened (or white) chocolate, chopped into chunks

several baking trays, greased

Makes 16

In a heatproof bowl, gently melt the 5 oz. chopped chocolate over a pan of barely simmering water. Remove from the heat and let cool.

Meanwhile beat the butter until creamy using a wooden spoon or electric mixer. Add the sugars and beat again until light and fluffy. Gradually beat in the egg and vanilla extract, followed by the melted chocolate.

Sift the flour into the bowl with the salt and baking powder and stir. When thoroughly combined, work in the chopped nuts and chocolate chunks.

Put heaped tablespoons of dough, spaced well apart, onto the prepared baking trays.

Bake in a preheated oven at 350°F for about 12 to 15 minutes until just firm. Cool for a couple of minutes until firm enough to transfer to a wire rack to cool completely.

Store in an airtight container. Eat within 1 week or freeze for up to 1 month.

squillionaire's
shortbread

14 oz. canned condensed milk

1 stick (½ cup) sweet butter,
at room temperature

5 tablespoons sugar

1 cup plus 1 tablespoon
all-purpose flour

3 tablespoons unsweetened cocoa

Chocolate Topping:

6 oz. bittersweet chocolate

2 tablespoons sweet butter, diced

about 2 oz. white chocolate,
to finish

one square, 9-inch cake pan,
2 inches deep, greased

Makes 16

To make the filling, put the unopened can of condensed milk in a heavy pan and cover with water. Bring to a boil, then simmer without covering the pan for 3½ hours. Top up the water regularly: the can must always be covered. Cool the can completely before opening. The condensed milk should have become a fudgy, dark, golden caramel.

Meanwhile, to make the chocolate cookie base, beat the butter until creamy, then beat in the sugar. When the mixture is light and fluffy, sift the flour with the cocoa into the bowl and work with your hands to make a smooth dough. Press the dough into the prepared cake pan to make an even layer. Prick well with a fork and chill for 15 minutes.

Bake the cookie base in a preheated oven at 350°F for 20 minutes until just firm and slightly darker around the edges—do not overcook or it will taste bitter.

Let cool in the pan. When completely cold, spread the cold caramel over the top. Chill until firm—about 1 to 2 hours.

To make the topping, chop the chocolate and melt in a heatproof bowl set over a pan of barely simmering water. Remove from the heat and stir in the butter. When smooth, spread over the caramel, then leave to set. Melt the white chocolate in the same way, then drizzle over the top of the dark chocolate using a fork or a wax paper frosting bag. Leave overnight until firm, then cut. Store in an airtight container and eat within 1 week. Not suitable for freezing.

three-chocolate
squares

Chop the chocolate and melt gently in a heatproof bowl set
over a pan of barely simmering water. Stir occasionally.
Remove the bowl from the heat and let cool.
Meanwhile beat the butter until creamy with a wooden spoon
or electric mixer. Add the sugar and vanilla and beat well.
Gradually beat in the egg, followed by the cooled chocolate.
Sift the flour with the baking powder, baking soda, and cocoa
into another bowl.
Using a metal spoon, fold the flour mixture into the chocolate
mixture in 3 batches alternating with the sour cream.
When thoroughly combined, spoon into the prepared pan and
smooth the surface.
Bake in a preheated oven at 375°F until just firm—about 25 to
30 minutes. Let cool in the pan before turning out.
To make the topping, melt the white chocolate as before, then
stir in the butter. When smooth, spread over the cake and
leave until set.
Cut into 16 pieces and store in an airtight container. Eat
within 5 days or freeze for up to 1 month.

Three kinds of chocolate—white, bittersweet, and cocoa—make great treats, good with coffee.

2½ oz. bittersweet chocolate

1 stick (½ cup),
at room temperature

¾ cup plus 1 tablespoon light
brown sugar

½ teaspoon real vanilla extract

1 large egg, beaten

1½ cups all-purpose flour

1 teaspoon baking powder

½ teaspoon baking soda

¼ cup unsweetened cocoa

⅓ cup sour cream

White Chocolate Topping:

2 oz. good quality white
chocolate, chopped

1½ tablespoons sweet butter,
at room temperature

one square, 8-inch cake pan,
greased and lined with
baking parchment

Makes 16

fudge brownies

1¼ sticks (½ cup plus 2 tablespoons) sweet butter

4 large eggs, beaten

1¾ cups light brown sugar

1 teaspoon real vanilla extract

a good pinch of salt

¾ cup unsweetened cocoa

1 cup minus 1 tablespoon all-purpose flour

3½ oz. walnut or pecan pieces, chopped white or bittersweet chocolate, or a combination

one square, 9-inch cake pan, 2 inches deep, completely lined with foil

Makes 16

Gently melt the butter in a pan and let cool while preparing the rest of the mixture.

Using a wooden spoon, beat the eggs very gently with the sugar until just blended and free of lumps. Stir in the cooled butter and the vanilla. Sift the salt, cocoa, and flour together into the bowl and gently stir in—do not beat or overmix, or the brownies will become cake-like.

When combined, fold in the nuts or chocolate. Pour into the prepared pan and smooth the surface.

Bake in a preheated oven at 325°F for about 35 to 40 minutes or until a skewer inserted midway between the center and the side of the pan comes out clean. The center should be just firm—do not overcook or the brownies will be dry.

Put the pan on a damp cloth to cool completely.

Lift the brownies out of the pan still in the foil, remove the foil, and cut into 16 squares.

Store in an airtight container and eat within 1 week or freeze for up to 1 month.

A wonderful version of one of the great **American** classics.

blondies

1¼ sticks (½ cup plus 2 tablespoons) sweet butter

2 cups light brown sugar

1 teaspoon real vanilla extract

3 large eggs, beaten

2 cups all-purpose flour

1 teaspoon baking powder

a large pinch of salt

2 oz. walnut pieces, coarsely chopped

2 oz. good white chocolate, coarsely chopped

2 oz. bittersweet chocolate, coarsely chopped

one 12 x 8½ inch roasting or baking pan, lined with foil

Makes 48

Put the butter into a large, heavy saucepan and melt gently. Add the sugar, stir well, then remove from the heat. Cool for 1 minute, then stir in the vanilla extract and the eggs.

Sift the flour, baking powder, and salt into the saucepan and stir just until thoroughly blended—do not beat or overmix.

Pour the mixture into the prepared baking pan and spread evenly. Sprinkle the nuts and chopped chocolate over the top. Bake in a preheated oven at 350°F for about 25 minutes until just firm.

Cool for a few minutes in the pan then lift the cake, still in the foil, onto a wire rack to cool completely.

Remove the foil and cut into 48 squares. Store in an airtight container and eat within 4 days. They can be frozen for up to 1 month, but they will be stickier than freshly baked ones.

Pale-gold brownies, topped **with nuts and two kinds of chocolate—dark** and **white.**

A *delicate* mixture flavored with finely ground coffee.
mocha madeleines

Chop the chocolate and melt gently with the butter in a heatproof bowl set over a pan of barely simmering water, stirring frequently. Remove from the heat and let cool. Meanwhile, sift the flour twice with the cocoa, salt, and coffee, then set aside. Using an electric mixer, beat the eggs with the sugar until the mixture becomes pale and thick—when the beater is lifted out, the mixture should leave a ribbon like trail on the surface.

Using a large metal spoon, fold the flour mixture into the egg mixture in 3 batches, then carefully fold in the chocolate mixture until all are thoroughly combined (the mixture will lose a little bulk).

Put a heaped teaspoon or so of the mixture into each madeleine mold so it is two-thirds full.

Bake in a preheated oven at 375°F for about 10 to 12 minutes or until just firm. Let cool for 1 minute, then remove from the molds using a table knife.

Cool on a wire rack, then dust with confectioners' sugar. Store in an airtight container and eat within 1 week or freeze for up to 1 month.

Note: *Non-stick madeleine molds work best. If using ordinary metal molds, brush them with 2 coats of melted butter and chill between applications.*

3 oz. bittersweet chocolate

1¼ sticks (½ cup plus 2 tablespoons) sweet butter, diced

1 cup minus 1 tablespoon all-purpose flour

2 tablespoons unsweetened cocoa

a pinch of salt

1 teaspoon finely ground espresso coffee

4 large eggs

¾ cup minus 1 tablespoon sugar

confectioners' sugar, for dusting

madeleine molds, twice-buttered

Makes 30

chocolate pear tart

1 cup plus 3 tablespoons
all-purpose flour

1 stick (½ cup) sweet butter,
chilled and diced

2½ tablespoons sugar

1 egg yolk

about 1 tablespoon ice water

Chocolate Pear Filling:

4½ oz. bittersweet chocolate,
chopped

1 stick (½ cup), plus 1 tablespoon
sweet butter, at room temperature

7 tablespoons sugar

4 large eggs, separated

1¼ cups plus 2 tablespoons
ground almonds

2–3 drops real almond extract

a pinch of salt

2 ripe medium-sized pears

one deep, 9-inch
false-bottom tart pan

one baking tray

Makes 1 tart, serves 8

To make the pastry, sift the flour into a bowl, and rub in the diced butter with the tips of your fingers until the mixture resembles fine crumbs.

Stir in the sugar, add the egg yolk and water, then bind the mixture together using a table knife or pastry blender. If the dough is dry and crumbly, add a little extra water.

Without kneading, quickly bring the dough together with your hands to make a soft but not sticky ball.

To make the dough in a food processor, put the flour, butter, and sugar into the bowl and process until the mixture resembles fine crumbs. With the machine running, add the yolk and water through the feed tube and process just until the dough comes together.

Wrap and chill the dough for 20 minutes. On a lightly floured surface, roll out the pastry to a circle 11½ inches across. Line the tart pan with it. Chill while preparing the filling.

Put a baking tray into a preheated oven 400°F to heat up—this helps to make the tart shell crisp.

To make the filling, very gently melt the chocolate in a heatproof bowl set over a pan of barely simmering water. Stir until smooth, then remove from the heat and let cool.

Meanwhile, using an electric mixer or wooden spoon, beat the butter until creamy, then beat in the sugar. When the mixture is light and fluffy, beat in the egg yolks one at a time, beating well after each addition. Beat in the cooled chocolate, then stir in the almonds and extract using a large metal spoon.

In a very clean greasefree bowl, beat the egg whites with the pinch of salt until they form soft peaks. Using a large metal spoon, gently fold them into the chocolate mixture in 3 batches. Spoon into the prepared chilled tart shell and spread evenly.

Peel and halve the pears, then scoop out the cores with a melon-baller or pointed teaspoon. Thinly slice the pear halves, leaving the slices attached at the stalk end, so they resemble fans. Arrange the pears on top of the chocolate mixture in a neat pattern.

Set the tart pan on the heated baking tray and bake for 15 minutes, then reduce the oven temperature to 350°F and bake for about 10 minutes longer or until just cooked in the center—test with a skewer.

Very carefully unmold and serve either warm or at room temperature with crème fraîche or vanilla ice-cream. The tart tastes better the day after baking, though it sinks slightly.

Variation:

Chocolate Normandy Tart

Substitute crisp, tart apples for the pears and prepare them in the same way. Add ½ teaspoon ground cinnamon to the chocolate filling, and proceed as in the main recipe.

Use just-ripe **Comice** pears for this **rich**, not-too-sweet tart.

Serve warm, at room temperature, or **chilled** *with vanilla ice cream, crème fraîche, or chocolate sauce.*

chestnut and chocolate moneybags

about 10½ oz. filo pastry

7 oz. bittersweet chocolate

1 cup plus 1 tablespoon curd cheese, such as ricotta

3 tablespoons dark brown sugar

2 egg yolks

2–3 tablespoons rum

4 oz. drained cooked chestnuts, roughly chopped (vacuum-packed or canned in light syrup or water)

½ stick (¼ cup sweet butter, melted, for brushing

confectioners' sugar for dusting

several baking trays

Makes 12, serves 4–6

If necessary defrost the pastry according to the package instructions. (Filo varies enormously between brands—some are very good: others turn out tough and leathery. Ask advice from other cooks about the best local brands.)

To make the filling, grate the chocolate coarsely and set aside. Beat the curd cheese until softened using a wooden spoon, then beat in the sugar followed by the egg yolks. Add rum to taste. Using a metal spoon, gently stir in the grated chocolate and the chestnuts.

Remove the pastry from the box and cover with a damp cloth until ready to use—the sheets of dough dry out very easily and become unusable. Put 3 sheets on a work surface and cut into 7-inch squares. Put a heaped tablespoon of the mixture (¹⁄₁₂ of the amount) into the center of each square, gather up the edges, and twist the top to resemble a pastry money bag. There is no need to dampen the edges of the pastry. Repeat to make 12. Arrange, spaced well apart on the baking trays and chill for about 15 minutes.

Brush with melted butter, then bake in a preheated oven at 375°F for about 15 minutes until golden brown. Serve, dusted with confectioners' sugar.

southern deep-dish
pecan pie

1 cup plus 3 tablespoons
all-purpose flour

a pinch of salt

1 stick (½ cup) sweet butter,
chilled and diced

2½ tablespoons sugar

1 egg yolk

1 tablespoon ice water, to bind

Pecan Filling:

1 cup plus 1½ tablespoons
light brown sugar

1¼ cups heavy cream

2½ oz. bittersweet chocolate,
chopped

2 egg yolks

½ teaspoon real vanilla extract

1 tablespoon bourbon (optional)

1½ cups pecan halves

shaved or grated white chocolate
"curls", to finish

one false-bottom, deep,
9-inch tart pan

Makes 1 pie, serves 8–10

If using a food processor, put the flour and salt into the bowl. Add the butter and process until fine crumbs are formed. Add the sugar and process briefly. With the machine running, add the egg yolk and water and process until the dough comes together. Wrap and chill for 20 minutes until firm.

Roll out the dough to a large circle about 11½ inches across and use to line the tart pan. Prick well and chill for about 15 minutes.

To bake the pastry blind, fill with a round of parchment paper and baking beans and cook in a preheated oven at 400°F for about 15 minutes until firm. Remove the paper and beans and return the pie shell, still in its pan, to the oven for about 5–10 minutes until crisp and golden. Let cool.

To prepare the filling, put the sugar and cream into a heavy pan and stir over medium heat until the sugar has melted and the mixture is almost boiling. Remove from the heat and stir in the chocolate. When smooth add the egg yolks and mix well. Stir over very low heat until the mixture thickens. Remove from the heat and stir in the vanilla, bourbon (if using), and nuts. Pour into the prepared pie shell and chill until firm. Serve decorated with white chocolate curls (these are made using a vegetable peeler or grater).

A pecan pie with **nuts**, chocolate, and **bourbon.**

amaretti chocolate
cheesecake pie

To make the crust, mix the butter and crushed amaretti crumbs then press onto the base of the prepared pan in an even layer. Chill while making the filling.

To make the filling, chop the chocolate and melt it gently in a heatproof bowl set over a pan of steaming water. Remove from the heat, stir until smooth, then let cool.

Put the cream cheese, eggs, and sugar into the bowl of a food processor and process until thoroughly combined. Add the cream and process again until just mixed. With the machine running add the melted chocolate and amaretto, if using, through the feed tube, and process until smooth.

Spoon the filling into the prepared pan and smooth the surface. Bake in a preheated oven at 325°F for 40 minutes until firm. Let cool in the oven with the door ajar. When completely cold, chill overnight.

Unclip the pan and remove the cheesecake. Decorate the top with the broken amaretti cookies. Drizzle with the melted chocolate, using either a wax paper frosting bag with the end snipped off, or a fork dipped in the chocolate.

Store the cheesecake in a covered container in the fridge then remove 30 minutes before serving. Eat within 5 days or freeze for up to 1 month.

Amaretti add crunchy texture and nutty taste to this easy recipe.

½ stick (¼ cup) sweet butter, melted

3½ oz. amaretti cookies, crushed, plus 6 extra, broken, to finish

1½ oz. bittersweet chocolate, melted, to drizzle

Chocolate Filling:

7 oz. bittersweet chocolate

1¾ cups cream cheese

2 eggs

5 tablespoons sugar

⅞ cup heavy cream

¼ cup amaretto liqueur (optional)

one 8½-inch springform pan, greased

Serves 12

A thoroughly **self-indulgent,** *grown-up version of a traditional English nursery pudding.*

chocolate
rice pudding

1 oz. bittersweet chocolate, chopped

2½ cups whole milk

2½ tablespoons short-grained rice

2 tablespoons superfine or granulated sugar

1 vanilla bean*

one 3-cup ovenproof baking dish, very well buttered

Serves 4

The vanilla bean can be rinsed carefully, dried, then used again.

Heat the chocolate and milk gently in a pan just until melted, stirring occasionally. Let cool. Put the rice, sugar, and vanilla bean in the buttered dish and pour in the chocolate milk. Stir gently, then bake in a preheated oven at 300°F for about 2½ hours until the rice is tender and the pudding thickened. Serve warm.

Variation:

Chocolate Rice Cream

This variation is cooked on top of the stove. Omit the vanilla bean and put the remaining ingredients in a saucepan with 3 green cardamom pods. Bring to a boil, stirring, then simmer for 40 minutes until the rice is soft. Remove the cardamom. Stir in 1 egg yolk and cook 1 minute. Pour into a large serving dish or small dishes, cool, cover, and chill. Serve ice cold, sprinkled with confectioners' sugar or a drizzle of cream.

hot white
chocolate pudding

Melt the chopped chocolate in a heatproof bowl set over a pan of barely simmering water. Remove from the heat and stir until smooth.

Using a wooden spoon or electric mixer, beat the butter until creamy, then gradually beat in the sugar. When the mixture is very light and fluffy, beat in the eggs, 1 tablespoon at a time, beating well after each addition.

Using a metal spoon, carefully fold in the flour and salt, then fold in the melted chocolate, vanilla extract, and enough milk to give a soft, dropping consistency.

Spoon into the prepared dish—it should be two-thirds full. Cover loosely with buttered foil and bake in a preheated oven at 350°F for about 35 minutes or until firm.

Meanwhile, to make the chocolate custard, heat the milk in a saucepan until scalding hot. Sift the cocoa, sugar, and cornstarch into a bowl and mix to a thick paste with the egg yolks and about 1 tablespoon of the milk. Stir in the remaining milk, then return the mixture to the pan. Stir over low heat until very hot, thickened, and smooth—do not allow to boil. Serve immediately with the pudding.

A cold weather *treat*—baked chocolate sponge pudding, served with chocolate *custard*.

3 oz. white chocolate, chopped

1 stick (½ cup) sweet butter, at room temperature

½ cup plus 1 tablespoon superfine or granulated sugar

2 large eggs, beaten

1 cup self-rising flour

a pinch of salt

a few drops real vanilla extract

about 3 tablespoons milk

Chocolate Custard:

1¾ cups whole milk

3 tablespoons unsweetened cocoa

4 tablespoons superfine or granulated sugar

2 tablespoons cornstarch

2 egg yolks

one 3-cup baking dish, well greased

Serves 4

A wonderfully *rich*, light, smooth *souffle with a surprise filling.*

rich chocolate soufflé

Brush melted butter inside the ramekins and sprinkle with superfine sugar. Stand on a baking tray or in a roasting pan. Put the chocolate and cream into a heavy-based pan. Set over very low heat and stir occasionally until melted. Remove from the heat and stir gently until smooth. Gently stir in the egg yolks, one at a time, then half the brandy or liqueur. Put the 5 egg whites into a very clean, grease-free bowl and beat until stiff peaks form. Sprinkle with the sugar and briefly beat again to make a smooth, stiff meringue. If you over-beat the meringue at this stage it will do more harm than good, and the end result will be less smooth.

The chocolate mixture should be just warm, so gently reheat it if necessary. Using a large metal spoon, mix in a little of the meringue to loosen the consistency. Pour the chocolate mixture on top of the meringue and gently fold together until thoroughly combined but not over-mixed.

Half-fill the prepared ramekins. Spoon the remaining brandy or liqueur over the amaretti cookies then put one in the center of each ramekin. Add the remaining mixture until the ramekins are full almost to the rim.

Bake in a preheated oven at 425°F for 8–10 minutes. Remove from the oven when they are barely set (the centers should be soft and wobble when gently shaken). Sprinkle with confectioners' sugar and serve immediately.

6 oz. bittersweet chocolate, broken into small squares

½ cup plus 1 tablespoon heavy cream

3 eggs, separated, plus 2 egg whites

4 tablespoons brandy or amaretto liqueur

3 tablespoons superfine or granulated sugar

4 amaretti cookies

confectioners' sugar, for sprinkling

four 1¼-cup ovenproof ramekin dishes, buttered and sugared (see method)

Serves 4

A velvety **smooth** *finale for a* **special** *dinner party—serve this terrine with very strong coffee.*

chocolate terrine

14 oz. bittersweet chocolate, coarsely chopped

½ cup plus 2 tablespoons unsweetened cocoa

3 tablespoons strong espresso coffee

2 tablespoons brandy

6 large eggs, at room temperature

½ cup sugar

1 cup heavy cream, chilled

one loaf pan, 8½ x 4½ x 3 inches deep, greased and lined with baking parchment

one bain-marie or roasting pan

Serves 8

Put the chopped chocolate into a heatproof bowl with the cocoa and coffee. Set over a pan of barely simmering water and melt gently, stirring frequently. Remove the bowl from the heat, stir in the brandy, and let cool.

Meanwhile put the eggs into the bowl of an electric mixer and beat until frothy. Add the sugar and beat until the mixture is pale and very thick—the beaters should leave a ribbon-like trail when lifted.

In another bowl, whip the cream until it holds a soft peak. Using a large metal spoon, gently fold the chocolate mixture into the eggs. When combined, fold in the whipped cream. Spoon the mixture into the prepared pan, then stand the pan in a bain-marie (a roasting pan half-filled with warm water). Bake in a preheated oven at 325°F for about 1 to 1¼ hours or until a skewer inserted into the center of the mixture comes out clean.

Remove from the oven, let cool in the bain-marie for about 45 minutes, then lift the pan out of the bain-marie and leave until completely cold.

Chill overnight then turn out. Serve dusted with confectioners' sugar. Store, well wrapped in the refrigerator, for up to 5 days.

*This dessert is very **rich**, so serve in **small** portions.*

chocolate brûlée

2¾ cups thick light cream or thin pouring heavy cream

1 vanilla bean, split

10½ oz. bittersweet chocolate, finely chopped

4 egg yolks

½ cup plus 1 tablespoon confectioners' sugar, sifted

about 3 tablespoons superfine or granulated sugar, for sprinkling

eight ⅔-cup ramekins

one bain-marie or roasting pan

Serves 8

In a heavy saucepan, heat the cream with the split vanilla bean until scalding hot but not boiling. Remove from the heat, cover, and leave to infuse for 15 minutes.

Lift out the vanilla bean and scrape the seeds into the cream with the tip of a small knife.

Stir the chocolate into the cream until melted and smooth. Put the egg yolks and confectioners' sugar into a medium-sized bowl, beat with a wooden spoon until well blended, then stir in the warm chocolate cream. When thoroughly combined, pour into the ramekin dishes.

Stand the dishes in a bain-marie (a roasting pan half-filled with warm water) and bake in a preheated oven at 350°F for about 30 minutes until just firm. Remove from the bain-marie and let cool. Cover and chill overnight or for up to 48 hours.

Sprinkle a little sugar over the tops, then put under a very hot broiler for just a few minutes to caramelize. A warning: if the ramekins are left for too long under the broiler the chocolate cream will melt. Serve within 1 hour.

screen. Messages appear instantly. Everyone in a chat room can read all the messages and send replies, unless the users "go private" and have an IM chat. Sometimes, cyberbullies post mean messages about someone in a chat room for everyone to read.

Blogs are another way bullies can get to victims. People can read and write about a person or topic by adding comments to the blog. Some cyberbullies post hateful remarks about others on blogs.

Bash boards are online bulletin boards where people post their thoughts and opinions about other people. Many bash board

Cyberbullying can go viral, which means a large number of people are aware of the bullying via the Internet. Being disrespectful is one of the most common forms of cyberbullying.

postings make fun of people. Some bullies put up rude cartoons, drawings, or photos of their targets.

ONLINE GAMING

Many teens enjoy online or interactive gaming. Online gaming can attract cyberbullies who might taunt and tease beginners as they learn the game. They may continue to harass someone who has responded to their initial attacks or pretend to be someone else and make up lies about teens or other gamers.

EXCLUSION

A teen can be bullied without directly interacting with the bully. For example, a cyberbully might delete a teen from a friend's buddy list to make that teen feel left out. Or, a bully can lock someone out from everyone's messaging servers. The excluded person feels degraded and alone because of being isolated from the others.

A cyberbully might exclude a teen from Facebook, Myspace, Twitter, or other social networking sites. Bullies then build a community in which its members know what is going on in the victim's life. They might post hurtful e-messages, pictures, or videos about the teen victim.

CHAPTER 2

THE MANY FACES OF CYBERBULLIES

All cyberbullies have a reason for their behavior. Some may feel bad about themselves and think being a bully will help them feel better. Cyberbullies want to upset, hurt, or scare other people to feel superior and powerful. They want power over someone at any cost, or they seek a sense of control and attention by striking out at others. Using computers or cell phones allows them to reach their targets at any time. These electronic devices can also provide bullies a wider audience than only the target.

WHO ARE CYBERBULLIES?

Exactly who is a cyberbully is somewhat unknown because no single accepted definition of cyberbullying is in place in the United States. In addition, many people remain anonymous until caught. They can hide their identity by using temporary e-mail accounts and phony chat room names. The cyberbullies are then faceless, and victims can't see their real name, phone number, or address.

The majority of cyberbullies know their targets. They may crave having power over their targets, especially if they, too, are being bullied.

Cyberbullies are usually preteens and teens, although they can be people of any age. If savvy with technology, they can remain hidden while harming others. Most cyberbullies know their victim either in person or online. The target may be a classmate, a current or former friend, a relative, and so on. Some cyberbullies become familiar with their target from a chat room or online game. People might also cross the line with something they write or show on the Internet or a cell phone. Sometimes, what one person thinks is a joke could be insulting to someone else.

BYSTANDERS TO CYBERBULLYING

Bystanders are not bullies or victims, but they witness cyberbullying taking place. They may know it is wrong but not take any action to stop the bully or to help the victim. By their inaction, they give approval for the cyberbully to continue his or her improper behavior. For example, teens might pass around embarrassing e-mails, text messages, or IMs. Such actions openly encourage the bully who sent out the messages. Some people write nasty comments on a bash board that a bully has created. Other teens read rude e-mails and e-messages or look at embarrassing photos of someone but do not pass them on. However, by doing nothing, bystanders are part of the cyberbullying and are not being respectful and kind to the victims.

A number of factors or situations can increase the risk of a teen becoming a cyberbully. However, having one or more of these does not always mean that a teen will become a bully. Some factors that can have an effect include having poor self-control and poor parenting by caregivers, and feeling that it is OK to be cruel or violent. Abusing others is a way for some cyberbullies to cope with difficult situations at home, school, or work.

USING ELECTRONIC DEVICES

Knowing how cyberbullies work can help many teens deal with a bully. Cyberbullies do not physically hit or kick a target. With technology, they hurt people's feelings and make them feel unsafe and scared. When people think they cannot be seen or found out on the Internet, they may do things they would never do in person. Some teens mistakenly believe that bullying online is nothing serious. The ease of cyberbullying may appeal to them. People can instantly release put-downs, rumors, gossip, and embarrassing photos in e-mails, blogs, and chat rooms. For example, a girl might send a stream of nasty text messages to her former boyfriend

Teens who have disabilities are often targets of people who engage in bullying because they may be seen as being different from others.

after a painful break up. People can change electronic photos or videos to show something about an individual that is embarrassing or untrue. With a few clicks, one person can post hurtful words or pictures to a few or thousands of viewers.

Some cyberbullies know that using the Internet can make it difficult to trace and find them. Computers can easily allow people to be anonymous, enabling bullies to hurt their victims without seeing them in person. In addition, many teens are not supervised by adults when using the Internet or cell phones. This lack of attention can lead cyberbullies to feel that they can be hurtful to their victims and will not get caught by their parents or authorities.

By using the Internet and cell phones, bullies can get to teens at home, including evenings and weekends. They can attack repeatedly. Even if a bully stops, it may be difficult or impossible to remove all the mean online electronic messages or photos. Cyberbullies may not take down cruel photos or posts on Web sites or blogs when asked to do so.

FEMALE AND MALE CYBERBULLIES

Female and male teens tend to cyberbully in different ways. Girl cyberbullies prefer to share personal information about their targets. They are more likely to write mean and upsetting e-mails, IMs, and text messages. By spreading rumors and gossip, they can damage another teen's social life. Girls who bully usually harass victims on cell phones instead of on the Internet.

Boy cyberbullies more often make direct threats online to get revenge on someone else. They are more apt to tease and call their target names one-on-one. Boys typically use the computer to cyber-bully. For example, they might hack into a victim's computer and steal passwords. They tend to use their cell phones to pass around hurtful photos, drawings, or other images of their target. Boys, more than girls, use exclusion to cyberbully.

HURTFUL TO VICTIMS

All forms of cyberbullying are harmful to victims. Teens feel they cannot hide or have no way to escape from cyberbullies, even at home. They can be attacked online day or night, and they might not know what is being said about them or who is behind the cyberbull-ing. Targets might fear for their safety because of continual online threats and harassment.

Repeated bullying can cause victims to feel tense, afraid, and anxious. Teen victims might have more health problems, such as headaches, stomachaches, and colds. They can have mood diffi-culties and be hostile, angry, or irritable. Some cry often and easily. The self-esteem of victims may decrease, leading to feelings of worthlessness.

Some targets do not report cyberbullying and keep their prob-lem a secret. They think they can handle the taunts and teasing

Cyberbullying leaves no physical scars, but the hurt it causes can be very severe. Targets of cyberbullying often feel alone, which can lead to depression and anxiety.

themselves. Some feel weak and unpopular or are too embarrassed to speak up. Sometimes, they think they have done something wrong and worry they will be punished. Victims may fear revenge from their bullies. Another concern is that adults will not take their complaints seriously or will react in upsetting ways, such as taking away their cell phones or computers.

Such secrecy can cause teens to feel alone. The effects might be long lasting and can include depression, anxiety, drug abuse, and abuse of family members. Targets of cyberbullying may withdraw

and drop out of school activities, clubs, or sports teams, or not want to go to school. They lose interest in hobbies and friends, have low energy, and have difficulty concentrating and making decisions. Victims of cyberbullying might react by arriving at school very late or very early and avoiding school or activities. Sometimes, teen victims run away from home. Others feel that the only way out of their depression is to commit suicide.

MYTH   Cyberbullies are often popular, smart, and attractive.

FACT   Cyberbullies can be anyone, girls or boys, teens or adults. Everyone and anyone can be cyberbullied.

MYTH   Bystanders to cyberbullying are not affected in any way.

FACT   Many bystanders to cyberbullying do not feel good about themselves and can become troubled or sad. Bystanders, the bully, and the victim will not feel proud of their actions. All experience harm in some way when cyberbullying occurs.

MYTH   Most teens cyberbully to get revenge on someone.

FACT   Many teens think cyberbullying is funny or a way to play a joke on someone. Some teens cyberbully because they think their peers do it. Also, friends might encourage someone to cyberbully. Bullies may not realize the negative effects of their actions.

Myspace, Facebook, and many other online social networks allow teens to set up a profile to tell about themselves. Teens should not enter their age, phone number, home address, or school on their profile or other postings. They can choose an icon to use for profiles instead of posting personal photos. Online social networking, e-mail, and instant messaging sites allow teens to set limits on the people they can chat or message with by using privacy settings. Some online games also have privacy settings.

Teens need to be careful about the people they put on their friends and buddy lists. Friends can save, copy, rewrite, and repost whatever teens put on a social networking site, Web site, or blog. Teens should be responsible by asking if it is OK to post pictures of their friends.

CHOOSING STRONG USERNAMES AND PASSWORDS

Many e-mail, networking, and gaming sites ask people to choose a username and password. Having usernames and passwords that others cannot easily guess can protect against cyberbullies. Teens should not use their real names as their usernames because every-one on a site can see usernames.

A strong password is seven to sixteen characters in length and includes lower- and upper-case letters, numbers, punctuation marks, and other characters. Avoid passwords based on diction-ary terms, usernames, relative or pet names, telephone numbers, birthdays, and other information that may be readily known or easy to guess. To create a password, some teens think of an uncommon phrase or short sentence and take the first, second, or last letter of each word. They turn these letters into their password by adding

special characters near the beginning, middle, or end of the letters. Words, letters, or characters should not be repeated in a row, such as in the passwords "deskdesk" or "11B2wtt." Some Web sites tell how strong a password is when creating one. Following these instructions can help keep people safe.

If teens think that someone else knows their password, they should change it right away. People should not write down and keep their passwords where others can easily find them.

RESPONDING TO CYBERBULLIES

People deal with cyberbullying in different ways. Sometimes, they can take care of the cyberbullying on their own by ignoring the bully or deleting the bully's messages without reading them. Cyberbullies may give up if they do not get a response. Another option is to log off from e-mail or instant or text messaging, or shut off the cell phone. Changing usernames, e-mail addresses, or passwords might keep a bully away. Limiting computer and cell phone time is another good step. Teens may want to get a new cell phone number.

A bully can be blocked on e-mail sites, IM lists, Web sites, and social networking sites. Photos, pictures, and other images can also be blocked on e-mail sites. Teens should receive e-mails only from people in their address book or from people they know. When using a buddy list for IM or social network sites, people can be blocked based on their username. They can also be removed from a buddy list.

Sometimes, the real names of anonymous bullies can be figured out. Bullies tend to use the same words in person as they do online in their e-mails or messages. Their messages might include things they have done in person. That information provides clues about the identity of the bullies. Most cyberbullies are or were very close to the victim.

GETTING HELP

Some cyberbullies will not back down, causing teens to feel scared or distressed. However, they are not alone and can get help. Telling someone is important. Teens can tell a parent or another trusted adult, such as a relative, teacher, coach, guidance counselor, or youth group leader. People should never be afraid to speak up or feel cyberbullying is their fault. Teens should be honest about their experiences and any steps they have taken to deal with the bullies.

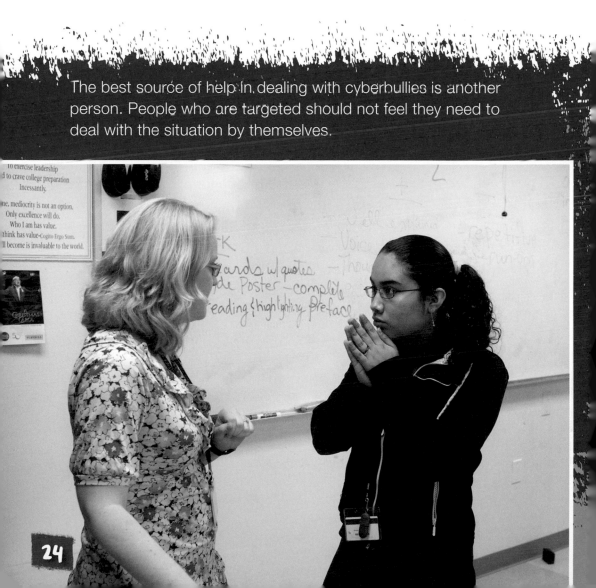

The best source of help in dealing with cyberbullies is another person. People who are targeted should not feel they need to deal with the situation by themselves.

Victims should not respond to cyberbullies. Instead, they can save any abusive or nasty e-mails, e-messages, and photos. They can print or forward the messages to an adult's phone. They can take screenshots to capture comments cyberbullies make in a chat room, an online gaming site, or a message board. Targets should also keep track of the date and time of a bully's activities in a journal or log. Recording the names of everyone who sends bullying messages is important because cyberbullies sometimes use several names.

Many schools post warning signs prohibiting bullying at the school or on school property. The signs are symbols demonstrating that teachers will help targets of cyberbullying if needed.

AT SCHOOL

If cyberbullied at school, students should report it. There might be a bullying box for reporting such incidents available at school. Students can explain the problem even when they do not know or want to say who the bullies are. Some schools have a bullying court that deals with bullying. Teachers and other staff members are usually not involved. Many schools have an antibullying policy and rules that discuss how it will deal with acts of bullying. The policy is available for all students at school and may also be available to read online. Guidance counselors are a good resource. They are trained to deal with bullying online, in school, and on school grounds.

INFORMING INTERNET SERVICE PROVIDERS

Bullies might change their e-mail address or not use their real name. Computer bullies often can be tracked down. All computers on the Internet have an Internet protocol (IP) address. An IP address usually is a set of four groups of numbers, such as 555.14.54.936.

An IP address is in the headers of e-mails. The header also includes information about the message, such as the identity of the sender, who received the message, the date and time the message was sent, and the subject of the message. The full header of e-mails is usually hidden. Teens or adults can determine the full header to find out the route the e-mail took to reach someone, including the original IP address of the cyberbullies.

Armed with this information, people can report bullies to their Internet service provider (ISP). ISPs host Web sites. They have rules about what people can and cannot do on Web sites. Adults can call or e-mail the ISP and ask them to deal with online bullies. People who have broken the rules can get booted off a site.

TELLING CHAT HOSTS

Teens who stick with chat rooms monitored by a person are provided with some safety. Usually the chat host checks the activities on the site to keep messages safe. The host polices the site and kicks off cyberbullies. Teens, though, need to report bullies. The messages between people are private, and the host cannot read them. It is up to teens to keep track of what cyberbullies write and then pass the information to the host.

HANDLING ONLINE GAME BULLIES

If bullies strike during online gaming, victims can stop playing the game for a while. They should also tell the people who run the game site about the cyberbullying. Some sites will allow teens to create a game to play only with invited players.

ENDING CELL PHONE HARASSMENT

Bullying by phone can take the form of nasty or silent phone calls or mean text messages. Teens can tell the abuser to stop calling or sending messages. Sometimes, the cyberbully is anonymous. Teens should keep all threatening messages and let a trusted adult know about them. The adult can contact the phone network. People there can find the bully's network and block the phone used to send the messages. The cyberbully's account can also be suspended from the phone network. Young people who are harassed by phone should make sure they seek professional help with an adult's assistance.

10 GREAT QUESTIONS
to ask a guidance counselor

1 What is the first thing I should do if I receive threatening e-mails or text messages?

2 When should I call the police if I receive threatening messages?

3 Is it OK to send a mean e-mail to someone who cyberbullies me?

4 Should I ignore someone who is cyberbullying me?

5 Is it OK to use my cell phone if someone is texting mean messages to me?

6 Can an anonymous cyberbully be traced?

7 A friend sent me a rude e-mail about a classmate. What should I do?

8 What should I do if I think a friend is being cyberbullied?

9 How do I know if I am being a tattletale when telling someone about a cyberbully?

10 How do I know if I'm being a cyberbully?

CHAPTER 4

CYBERBULLYING SOLUTIONS

In 2011, forty-seven states had antibullying laws. Some of these states have updated and improved their older antibullying laws to include cyberbullying. Although cyberbullying is a newer problem than bullying, it is getting increased attention from the government, schools, organizations, and the media.

CYBERBULLYING AND THE LAW

Congress has considered laws that would make cyberbullying a federal crime. One bill, known as the Megan Meier Cyberbullying Prevention Act, has been before Congress in 2009 and 2010, but it has not passed into law. The bill may be brought to Congress in the future.

Some U.S. states have laws against cyberbullying, such as California, New Jersey, Missouri, New York, Rhode Island, and Maryland. At least seven states have passed laws against cyber harrassment since 2007. California was one of the first states to pass legislation on cyberbullying. The law went into effect on January 1, 2009. Under the law, schools can discipline

Tyler Clementi apparently committed suicide shortly after he was secretly videotaped in his dorm room and the video was streamed online.

students for bullying others online. In addition, some cities have made online harassment a crime.

Since 2010, public schools in New Jersey must follow the Anti-Bullying Bill of Rights. Some people think it is the strongest such law in the United States. The law was created and passed, in part, because of Tyler Clementi, a student at Rutgers University's Piscataway, New Jersey, campus. Without asking permission, his roommate and another student used a Webcam to spy on Clementi and another man kissing in his dorm room and then streamed the video over the Internet. Clementi committed suicide soon afterward.

WHAT SCHOOLS ARE DOING ABOUT CYBERBULLYING

In some states, teachers are required to report bullying. However, schools usually have limited authority to handle cyberbullying if it occurs after school hours or off school grounds. If the cyberbullying is happening at school and is reported, school administrators

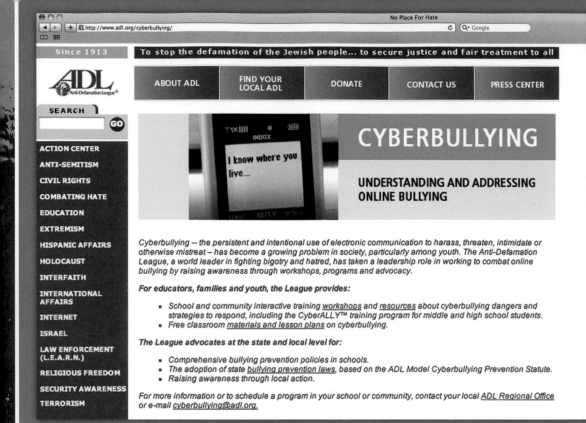

http://www.adl.org/cyberbullying/

Since 1913

To stop the defamation of the Jewish people... to secure justice and fair treatment to all

ADL
Anti-Defamation League®

ABOUT ADL

FIND YOUR LOCAL ADL

DONATE

CONTACT US

PRESS CENTER

SEARCH GO

ACTION CENTER

ANTI-SEMITISM

CIVIL RIGHTS

COMBATING HATE

EDUCATION

EXTREMISM

HISPANIC AFFAIRS

HOLOCAUST

INTERFAITH

INTERNATIONAL AFFAIRS

INTERNET

ISRAEL

LAW ENFORCEMENT (L.E.A.R.N.)

RELIGIOUS FREEDOM

SECURITY AWARENESS

TERRORISM

CYBERBULLYING

UNDERSTANDING AND ADDRESSING ONLINE BULLYING

Cyberbullying -- the persistent and intentional use of electronic communication to harass, threaten, intimidate or otherwise mistreat – has become a growing problem in society, particularly among youth. The Anti-Defamation League, a world leader in fighting bigotry and hatred, has taken a leadership role in working to combat online bullying by raising awareness through workshops, programs and advocacy.

For educators, families and youth, the League provides:

- School and community interactive training workshops and resources about cyberbullying dangers and strategies to respond, including the CyberALLY™ training program for middle and high school students.
- Free classroom materials and lesson plans on cyberbullying.

The League advocates at the state and local level for:

- Comprehensive bullying prevention policies in schools.
- The adoption of state bullying prevention laws, based on the ADL Model Cyberbullying Prevention Statute.
- Raising awareness through local action.

For more information or to schedule a program in your school or community, contact your local ADL Regional Office or e-mail cyberbullying@adl.org.

Through its Cyberbullying Resource Center, the Anti-Defamation League (ADL) and its Web site (www.adl.org) supply information about cyberbullying for teens, families, and communities.

probably will handle the situation. Peer counseling can be offered to the victim. If the cyberbullying escalates and becomes constant, the school may involve the parents so that they can work to stop the behavior. The bullies could be suspended or expelled from school. In serious situations, the police could become involved.

Some schools provide ongoing programs that help create a healthy social climate while students are in school. Kids at every grade level are taught how to be leaders and to be concerned about others. They also teach victims good ways of dealing with bullies.

Many schools are adopting bullying prevention programs that are provided by various organizations. One example is the Olweus Bullying Prevention Program by the Hazelden Foundation in Minnesota. Schools in many different countries have used this program for more than twenty years. The program focuses on preventing or reducing bullying at the school, classroom, and individual levels.

Another example is the Anti-Defamation League (ADL). This organization works throughout the world to raise awareness of bullying through technology. The ADL stresses that schools should have clear policies on cyberbullying that include training for all staff. In addition, the ADL promotes bullying prevention laws in all states.

Through the organization Students Against Violence Everywhere (SAVE), students learn cyberbullying information and prevention. Then they practice what they learn about nonviolence and conflict management skills through school and community service projects. For more than ten years, Web Wise Kids (WWK) has taught students and parents about the dangers of using the Internet and cell phones. WWK creates realistic and interactive computer games to reach teens and adults. To date, more than ten million middle and high school teens have been involved in WWK programs.

OTHER CYBERBULLYING RESOURCES

The Web site StopBullying.gov by the U.S. Department of Health and Human Services provides information from government agencies on how to prevent or stop bullying. It provides a list of resources for teens and their parents.

Sometimes, teens feel desperate about being cyberbullied and think they cannot talk to anyone. They may think about suicide because of their unbearable pain. Teens can call hotlines any time, day or night. All calls are confidential. The specially trained staff provides immediate support by listening to callers and discussing their

Cyberbullying has increased in recent years. Online information provided by the federal government at www.stopbullying.gov, and a growing number of organizations offer information on what cyberbullying is and how to stop it.

problems. If requested, staff can provide advice and tell teens where to go for more help. These hotlines are always open, and the call is free.

INDIVIDUAL RESPONSIBILITY

Even though the Internet may not feel like the real world, there are rules about how to behave online. If teens break these rules, they could lose their e-mail, IM, or Internet account. They could get into serious trouble with the law.

STOP BULLYING.
SAVE LIVES.

Seventeen-year-old John Otto spoke about his suffering through bullying.
He was with a group who stood outside the New Jersey State House as
lawmakers worked to toughen the state's antibullying laws.

Teens should make sure their e-messages are kind and respectful. One way to do this is to avoid gossiping, passing on or starting rumors, or harassing others online. When a person is feeling upset or angry over a message, it is a good idea for that person not to respond right away. Another idea is for teens to write a message and read it aloud to hear how it will sound to the reader. Or, they can count to ten and read their message again. Before pushing the send button, teens should try to picture the reader's reaction. They do not want the reader to feel angry, sad, or confused when seeing the message. In addition, teens should be careful before posting or sending messages or photos because those items could be used later by a bully to hurt them.

THE MEGAN MEIER CYBERBULLYING PREVENTION ACT

In 2006, thirteen-year-old Megan Meier of Dardenne Prairie, Missouri, had just started eighth grade and was on the school volleyball team. Megan met Josh Evans on Myspace and they quickly became online friends. In October, Josh started to send cruel e-mails to Megan. Soon mean bulletins about Megan were posted online. Deeply upset over the cyberbullying, the teen committed suicide three weeks before her fourteenth birthday. Megan's parents tried to message Josh, but his e-mail account had disappeared. Later, the police discovered that Josh was not real. The mother of one of Megan's former friends and another teen had made him up. Meier's story was widely reported on the Internet. On May 22, 2008, Linda T. Sanchez, U.S. representative from California, and Kenny Hulshof, U.S. representative from Missouri, cosponsored H.R. 6123, the Megan Meier Cyberbullying Prevention Act, to change the federal laws concerning cyberbullying. They introduced the bill hoping to make cyberbullying a federal offense that required cyberbullies to be fined and/or imprisoned for at most two years.

How each person acts on computers or cell phones is critical. People might want to say mean things to others online, especially if they get upset over a rude or embarrassing e-mail or e-message. Some teens may think it is fair to bully back. However, this reaction would only put another cyberbully on the Internet or cell phones. Teens can fight cyberbullying by joining the antiviolence programs at their school, community center, local clubs, or religious organizations. If their school or community does not have a program, they could ask a teacher or guidance counselor to organize classmates into an antibullying group or club. Although raising awareness about cyberbullying must start with the individual, antibullying clubs can provide concrete information about the dangers of cyberspace, the effects of bullying, and effective ways to combat cyberbullies.

anonymous Not identified by name; of unknown name.

assertive Having or showing a confident and forceful personality.

bash board An online bulletin board on which individuals can post anything they want. Generally, posts are hateful statements directed against another person.

block To deny access. A person blocked from joining a chat usually receives a message that says access has been denied.

blog A journal or diary published online instantly.

buddy list A collection of names or handles of friends or "buddies" within an instant-messaging or chat program.

bullying Hostile behavior or intentional harm done by one person or a group generally carried out repeatedly over time.

bystander A person who does not take part in an activity but watches or does not act to stop it.

chat An online conversation, typically carried out by people who use nicknames instead of their real names. A person can read messages from others in the chat room and type in and send in his or her own messages in reply.

chat room A virtual room where groups of people send and receive messages. All of the people in the room are listed by their screen names somewhere on the screen.

cyberbullying Intentionally harming somebody through electronic text or a technological device.

cyberstalking Repeatedly following a victim around chat rooms or repeatedly sending e-mails or text messages, or calling a victim so that the victim feels there is no escape.

cyber threat Message sent through the Internet or a cell phone that is intended to inflict harm or violence on someone else.

e-mail Electronic mail that allows Internet users to send and receive electronic text to and from other Internet users.

e-message An electronic or text message sent via the Internet or on a cell phone.

exclusion The act of not including someone in an online group, such as a buddy list.

harassment Words or actions intended to annoy, alarm, or abuse another individual.

hotline A telephone line that provides support for a particular type of problem.

instant messaging (IM) The act of Instantly communicating between two or more people over the Internet.

Internet A worldwide network of computers communicating with each other via phone lines, satellite links, wireless networks, and cable systems.

Internet service provider (ISP) A company that provides an Internet connection to individuals or companies.

self-esteem Confidence in one's own worth or abilities; self-respect.

social networking site An online service that brings people together by organizing them around a common interest and provides them with interactive photos, blogs, and messaging systems; examples include Facebook and Myspace.

spam Unsolicited electronic mail sent from someone the recipient does not know.

text message A written message sent by cell phone.

Kids' Internet Safety Alliance
WaterPark Place
20 Bay Street, 12th Floor, Suite 37
Toronto, ON M5J 2N8
Canada
(416) 850-1449
Web site: http://www.kinsa.net
The Kids' Internet Safety Alliance helps to protect children and
    teen victims of cyber abuse by educating the public, policy
    makers, and law enforcement.

Megan Meier Foundation
17295 Chesterfield Airport Road, Suite 200
Chesterfield, MO 63005
(636) 777-7823
Web site: http://meganmeierfoundation.cwsit.org
The Megan Meier Foundation teaches children, parents, and
    educators about the prevention of the bullying and cyberbully-
    ing of youth.

National Association of Students Against Violence Everywhere
322 Chapanoke Road, Suite 110
Raleigh, NC 27603
(866) 343-7283
Web site: http://www.nationalsave.org
This public nonprofit organization strives to decrease the potential
    for violence by engaging students in violence prevention efforts
    within their school and community.

PACER's National Bullying Prevention Center
8161 Normandale Boulevard
Bloomington, MN 55437
(888) 248-0822
Web site: http://www.pacer.org/bullying
PACER's National Bullying Prevention Center unites, engages, and educates communities nationwide to address bullying through creative, relevant, and interactive resources. This organization has named October as the National Bullying Prevention Month.

United States Department of Health and Human Services
200 Independence Avenue SW
Washington, DC 20201
(877) 696-6775
Web site: http://www.stopbullying.gov
StopBullying.gov provides information from various government agencies on how children, teens, parents, educators, and others in the community can prevent or stop bullying.

United States Department of Justice
950 Pennsylvania Avenue NW
Washington, DC 20530-0001
(202) 514-2000
Web site: http://www.justice.gov
The United States Department of Justice provides information about cyberbullying and federal leadership in preventing and controlling crime.

HOTLINES

Anti-Cyberbullying Hotline, Boston Public Health Commission
(617) 534-5050
Boys Town National Hotline (800) 448-3000
CrisisLink (888) 644-5886
Kids Help Hotline (Canada) (800) 668-6868
KUTO (Kids Under Twenty-One) Crisis Help (888) 644-5886
National Suicide Hotline (800) 784-2433
National Suicide Prevention Lifeline (800) 273-8255
National Youth Crisis Hotline (800) 448-4663
Teen Line (800) 852-8336
Trevor Lifeline for Gay, Lesbian, and Bisexual Youth (866) 488-7386
24-Hour Addiction Helpline (877) 579-0078
Youth America Hotline (877) 968-8454

WEB SITES

Due to the changing nature of Internet links, Rosen Publishing has developed an online list of Web sites related to the subject of this book. This site is updated regularly. Please use this link to access the list:

http://www.rosenlinks.com/beat/cyber

FOR FURTHER READING

Allman, Toney. *Mean Behind the Screen: What You Need to Know About Cyberbullying*. Mankato, MN: Compass Point Books, 2009.

Bott, Christie Jo. *More Bullies in More Books*. Lanham, MD: Scarecrow Press, 2009.

Breguet, Teri. *Frequently Asked Questions About Cyberbullying*. New York, NY: Rosen Publishing Group, Inc., 2007.

Casanova, Mary. *Chrissa Stands Strong*. Middleton, WI: American Girl, 2009.

Cindrich, Sharon Miller. *A Smart Girl's Guide to the Internet: How to Connect with Friends, Find What You Need, and Stay Safe Online*. Middleton, WI: American Girl, 2009.

Conifer, Dave. *eBully*. Charleston, SC: CreateSpace, 2010.

Criswell, Patti Kelley. *Stand Up for Yourself & Your Friends: Dealing with Bullies and Bossiness, and Finding a Better Way*. Middleton, WI: American Girl, 2009.

Fox, Dan. *Bullying and Hazing*. Farmington Hills, MI: Greenhaven Press, 2008.

Friedman, Lauri S., ed. *Bullying: An Opposing Viewpoints Guide*. Farmington Hills, MI: Greenhaven Press, 2011.

Friedman, Lauri S. *Cyberbullying*. Farmington, Hills, MI: Greenhaven Press, 2010.

Green, Susan Eikov. *Don't Pick On Me*. Oakland, CA: New Harbinger Publications, 2010.

Guillain, Charlotte. *Coping with Bullying*. Chicago, IL: Heinemann Library, 2011.

Hunter, Nick. *Cyber Bullying*. Chicago, IL: Heinemann Library, 2012.

Jacobs, Thomas A. *Teen Cyberbullying Investigated: Where Do Your Rights End and Consequences Begin?* Minneapolis, MN: Free Spirit Publishing, 2010.

Jakubiak, David J. *A Smart Kid's Guide to Online Bullying*. New York, NY: PowerKids Press, 2010.

Keene, Carolyn. *Secret Identity*. New York, NY: Aladdin, 2009.

MacEachern, Robyn. *Cyberbullying: Deal with It and Ctrl Alt Delete It*. Toronto, ON: Lorimer, 2011.

McQuade, Samuel, and Marcus K. Rogers. *Cyberstalking and Cyberbullying*. New York, NY: Chelsea House Publishers, 2011.

McQuade, Samuel, and Marcus K. Rogers. *Living with the Internet*. New York, NY: Chelsea House Publishers, 2011.

Simmons, Danette. *Teen Reflections: My Life, My Journey, My Story*. Charleston, SC: CreateSpace, 2010.

BIBLIOGRAPHY

American Academy of Pediatrics. *CyberSafe: Protecting and Empowering Kids in the Digital World of Texting, Gaming, and Social Media.* Elk Grove Village, IL: American Academy of Pediatrics, 2011.

Beane, Allan L. *Protect Your Child from Bullying: Expert Advice to Help You Recognize, Prevent, and Stop Bullying Before Your Child Gets Hurt.* San Francisco, CA: Jossey-Bass, 2008.

Canada Safety Council. "Cyber Bullying." October 19, 2010. Retrieved September 16, 2011 (http://canadasafetycouncil.org/news/cyber-bullying).

Centers for Disease Control and Prevention. "Electronic Aggression: Technology and Youth Violence." August 30, 2011. Retrieved September 12, 2011 (http://www.cdc.gov/ViolencePrevention/youthviolence/electronicaggression).

Hinduja, Sameer, and Justin W. Patchin. "Cyberbullying and Suicide." 2010. Retrieved September 14, 2011 (http://www.cyberbullying.us/cyberbullying_and_suicide_research_fact_sheet.pdf).

Hinduja, Sameer, and Justin W. Patchin. "Cyberbullying: Identification, Prevention, and Response." 2010. Retrieved September 15, 2011 (http://www.cyberbullying.us/Cyberbullying_Identification_Prevention_Response_Fact_Sheet.pdf).

Hinduja, Sameer, and Justin W. Patchin. "State Cyberbullying Laws." September 2011. Retrieved October 1, 2011. (http://www.cyberbullying.us/Cyberbullying_Identification_Prevention_Response_Fact_Sheet.pdf).

Hu, Winnie. "Bullying Law Puts New Jersey Schools on the Spot." *New York Times*, August 30, 2011. Retrieved August 31, 2011

(http://www.nytimes.com/2011/08/31/nyregion/bullying-law-puts-new-jersey-schools-on-spot.html?pagewanted=all).

Kowalski, Robin M., and Susan P. Limber. "Electronic Bullying Among Middle School Students." *Journal of Adolescent Health*, 2007. Retrieved September 2, 2011 (http://www.jahonline.org/webfiles/images/journals/jah/zaq11207000S22.pdf).

Lenhart, Amanada. "Cyberbullying." 2011. Retrieved September 12, 2011 (http://www.pewinternet.org/Reports/2007/Cyberbullying.aspx).

McQuade, Samuel C., James P. Colt, and Nancy B. B. Meyer. *Cyber Bullying: Protecting Kids and Adults from Online Bullies*. Westport, CT: Praeger Publishers, 2009.

Mulvihill, Geoff, and David Crary. "With Teen's Suicide Comes Spotlight, Caution." *Wall Street Journal*, September 22, 2011. Retrieved September 29, 2011 (http://online.wsj.com/article/APfb480cb288524568a66de88e51692a31.html).

National Center for Mental Health Promotion and Youth Violence Prevention. "Preventing Cyberbullying in Schools and the Community." June 20, 2011. Retrieved September 25, 2011 (http://www.promoteprevent.org/publications/prevention-briefs/preventing-cyberbullying-schools-and-community).

National Crime Prevention Association. "Cyberbullying." 2001. Retrieved September 9, 2011 (http://www.ncpc.org/cyberbullying).

OnGuardOnline.gov. "Cyberbullying." September 2011. Retrieved September 25, 2011 (http://onguardonline.gov/articles/0028-cyberbullying).

OnGuardOnline.gov. "Kids and Socializing Online." September 2011. Retrieved September 25, 2011 (http://onguardonline.gov/articles/0012-kids-and-socializing-online).

OnGuardOnline.gov. "Kids and Virtual Worlds." September 2011. Retrieved September 25, 2011 (http://onguardonline.gov/articles/0030-kids-and-virtual-worlds).

Rogers, Vanessa. *Cyberbullying: Activities to Help Children and Teens to Stay Safe in a Texting, Twittering, Social Networking World*. Philadelphia, PA: Jessica Kingsley Publishers, 2010.

Shariff, Shaheen, and Andrew W. Churchill. *Truths and Myths of Cyber-Bullying*. New York, NY: Peter Lang Publishing, 2009.

Willard, Nancy. "Educator's Guide to Cyberbullying and Cyberthreats." Center for Safe and Responsible Internet Use, April 2007. Retrieved September 15, 2011 (http://csriu.org/cyberbully/docs/cbcteducator.pdf).

INDEX

ABOUT THE AUTHOR

Judy Monroe Peterson has earned two master's degrees and is the author of more than sixty educational books for young people. She is a former health care, technical, and academic librarian and college faculty member; a biologist and research scientist; and curriculum editor with more than twenty-five years of experience. She has taught courses at 3M, the University of Minnesota, and Lake Superior College. Currently, she is a writer and editor of K–12 and post–high school curriculum materials on a variety of subjects, including biology, life science, and the environment.

PHOTO CREDITS

Cover © istockphoto.com/Derek Latta; p. 5 © Rawdon Wyatt/Alamy; p. 8 Brendan O'Sullivan/Photolibrary/Getty Images; p. 9 Andrew Bret Walli/Photographer's Choice RF/Getty Images; p. 11 istockphoto.com/Carri Keill; p. 14 istockphoto.com/Kurt Gordon; p. 16 Lisa F. Young/Shutterstock; p. 18 Peter Close/Shutterstock; p. 21 Allison Long/MCT/Newscom; p. 24 © Bob Daemmrich/The Image Works; p. 25 © Rob Nelson/PhotoEdit; p. 30 Emmanuel Dunand/AFP/Getty Images; p. 31 Reprinted with permission, New York: Anti-Defamation League, © 2011, www.adl.org, all rights reserved; p. 34 © AP Images; back cover background, interior graphics © istockphoto.com/aleksandar velasevic.

Designer: Nicole Russo; Editor: Kathy Kuhtz Campbell;
Photo Researcher: Marty Levick

DATE DUE

NOV 2 0 2012

NOV 2 0 2016

PRINTED IN U.S.A.